Empathy and Compasssion

CAUSES & EFFECTS OF EMOTIONS

CAUSES & EFFECTS OF EMOTIONS

Empathy and Compasssion

Rosa Waters

Mason Crest

Mason Crest
450 Parkway Drive, Suite D
Broomall, PA 19008
www.masoncrest.com

Printed and bound in the United States of America.

First printing
9 8 7 6 5 4 3 2 1

Series ISBN: 978-1-4222-3067-1
ISBN: 978-1-4222-3071-8
ebook ISBN: 978-1-4222-8764-4

The Library of Congress has cataloged the
hardcopy format(s) as follows:
        Library of Congress Cataloging-in-Publication Data

Waters, Rosa, 1957-
  Empathy and compassion / Rosa Waters.
      pages cm. — (Causes & effects of emotions)
  ISBN 978-1-4222-3071-8 (hardback)
  1. Empathy in children—Juvenile literature. 2. Empathy—Juvenile litera-
ture. 3. Compassion in children—Juvenile literature. 4. Compassion—
Juvenile literature. I. Title.
  BF723.E67W38 2015
  152.4'1—dc23
                                                2014004380

CONTENTS

KEY ICONS TO LOOK FOR:

Text-Dependent Questions: These questions send the reader back to the text for more careful attention to the evidence presented there.

Words to Understand: These words with their easy-to-understand definitions will increase the reader's understanding of the text, while building vocabulary skills.

Series Glossary of Key Terms: This back-of-the book glossary contains terminology used throughout this series. Words found here increase the reader's ability to read and comprehend higher-level books and articles in this field.

Research Projects: Readers are pointed toward areas of further inquiry connected to each chapter. Suggestions are provided for projects that encourage deeper research and analysis.

Sidebars: This boxed material within the main text allows readers to build knowledge, gain insights, explore possibilities, and broaden their perspectives by weaving together additional information to provide realistic and holistic perspectives.

INTRODUCTION

The journey of self-discovery for young adults can be a passage that includes times of introspection as well joyful experiences. It can also be a complicated route filled with confusing road signs and hazards along the way. The choices teens make will have lifelong impacts. From early romantic relationships to complex feelings of anxiousness, loneliness, and compassion, this series of books is designed specifically for young adults, tackling many of the challenges facing them as they navigate the social and emotional world around and within them. Each chapter explores the social emotional pitfalls and triumphs of young adults, using stories in which readers will see themselves reflected.

Adolescents encounter compound issues today in home, school, and community. Many young adults may feel ill equipped to identify and manage the broad range of emotions they experience as their minds and bodies change and grow. They face many adult problems without the knowledge and tools needed to find satisfactory solutions. Where do they fit in? Why are they afraid? Do others feel as lonely and lost as they do? How do they handle the emotions that can engulf them when a friend betrays them or they fail to make the grade? These are all important questions that young adults may face. Young adults need guidance to pilot their way through changing feelings that are influenced by peers, family relationships, and an ever-changing world. They need to know that they share common strengths and pressures with their peers. Realizing they are not alone with their questions can help them develop important attributes of resilience and hope.

The books in this series skillfully capture young people's everyday, real-life emotional journeys and provides practical and meaningful information that can offer hope to all who read them.

It covers topics that teens may be hesitant to discuss with others, giving them a context for their own feelings and relationships. It is an essential tool to help young adults understand themselves and their place in the world around them—and a valuable asset for teachers and counselors working to help young people become healthy, confident, and compassionate members of our society.

Cindy Croft, M.A.Ed
Director of the Center for Inclusive Child Care at Concordia University

Words to Understand

psychologists: People who are experts on emotions and the human mind.

sociologists: People who study societies and how humans interact.

cognitive: Having to do with the mind or knowledge.

manipulate: To control or influence a person to do what you want.

perspective: Understanding of what's really important.

capacity: The ability to do something.

ONE

WHAT ARE EMPATHY AND COMPASSION?

Imagine your best friend comes to you in tears. She tells you that her boyfriend just broke up with her—but he didn't just break up; he also told her that he thought she was a mean, ugly person, and he doesn't know what he ever saw in her. Your friend is heartbroken.

How do you feel?

Or suppose that you're watching television and a news story comes on about something terrible that's happening in Africa. You see pictures of starving, crying children. What really gets to you is that one of the little boys on the screen reminds you of your little brother.

How do you feel?

Next, pretend you're on the school bus. There's a kid no one likes who rides your bus. No one ever sits with him. And today,

EMPATHY AND COMPASSION

Sometimes a child's first experiences with empathy and compassion may be with an animal.

a bunch of kids are making fun of him. He's hunched down in his seat, looking miserable. You don't want to look at him, but something makes you meet his eyes. When you do, you see that his eyes are full of tears.

How do you feel?

What do you do?

FEELING FOR OTHERS

What you probably felt in each of these situations was something that felt like emotional pain. Another person's pain made you hurt too. Psychologists call these feelings empathy and compassion. Empathy and compassion are a lot alike, but they're also a little different from each other.

Make Connections

Empathy and compassion are just one kind of emotion. They're a lot like love and affection, not so much like anger and hatred. But all emotions, positive and negative, have some things in common. Our feelings take place in our brains. Scientists say that all emotions are impulses within our brain cells that move us to action. Our emotions are triggered by something outside us—and then they prompt us to behave in certain ways. Those behaviors include smiling, shouting, laughing, and crying. They also include getting in fights—and reaching out to help another person. Humans developed emotions because in one way or another, they helped us survive. Being happy or sad, angry or surprised, compassionate or jealous—those are all survival mechanisms.

Empathy

Empathy comes from Greek words that meant simply "in feeling," "in an emotional state," or "feeling into." Emotion researchers have added on to that most basic definition. **Psychologists** and **sociologists** generally define empathy as the ability to sense other people's emotions. People with empathy are able to imagine what someone else might be thinking or feeling. They recognize and understand another's suffering. It's the feeling that allows them to "walk a mile in someone else's shoes."

Psychologists think empathy is connected to the ability to "catch" another person's emotions. We've all experienced that. When someone else laughs, it's easy to start laughing too. When we're with someone who's sad, we may start to feel down too. Even animals can pick up each other's emotions. In fact, many pets can even pick up their humans' emotions. But this isn't quite the same as empathy.

EMPATHY AND COMPASSION

When your friend's pain makes you cry too, you're experiencing empathy.

Make Connections

The Greek word *pathos* meant feeling. It's the root of *sympathy* (which came from roots that meant "together feeling") and *empathy* ("in feeling"). There's also a word that means "I don't care"—*apathy*. The root words of this word mean "without feeling."

If you start laughing when you see someone else laughing, you feel amused, even if you don't know why. You think the other person's laughter is funny. Amusement is *your* emotion. Now say, you start crying as you listen to your friend tell her story about her breakup with her boyfriend. In order for the feeling to be empathy, you have to see that your friend is in pain and share her pain, while at the same time you know that it's not your own emotion you're feeling. *You're* not the one who was hurt. The pain that you're feeling is for your friend, not for yourself.

Having empathy isn't always enough, though. It doesn't necessarily mean we'll do anything but feel bad. It doesn't mean we'll help the person who's hurting. Psychologist Paul Ekman, an expert on emotions research, says that there are actually three kinds of empathy—and only one of them will actually trigger us to take positive action.

The first form he calls *"cognitive empathy."* This means when you see someone who is hurting, you recognize what he's feeling. You saw the kid on the bus with tears in his eyes, and you could tell he was sad. You might use this knowledge to help—but you could also use it to *manipulate* the other person to your own advantage. Cognitive empathy can be selfish.

Which is why Ekman says we also need what he calls "emotional empathy"—when we physically feel what other people feel. But even this can have a downside. Say when you see the kid on the bus crying, you get so upset that you're a mess for the rest of the day. You don't want to talk to your friends. You can't focus

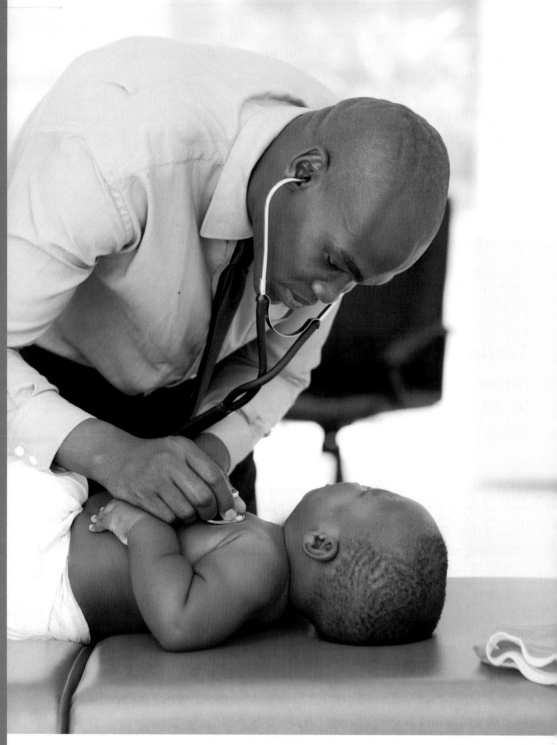

People in the helping professions need empathy—but they also need to protect themselves from caring so much that they burn out.

on your schoolwork. You're just too upset. You can't stop thinking about how sad the kid was. But your emotions aren't doing that kid on the bus a bit of good.

To do that we need what Ekman calls "compassionate empathy." With this kind of empathy we not only understand and feel a person's pain, but we are moved to take action. We help. Ekman says compassionate empathy springs from the knowledge that we're all connected. And it can lead to outbursts of what he calls "constructive anger." So say you're on the bus and people are being mean to the kid no one likes. You suddenly lose your temper. You tell off the bullies, and then you plop down in the seat next to the kid. "How are you doing?" you ask. "Did you get your math homework done?" This kind of compassionate empathy makes you reach out. It carries you from empathy to compassion.

Compassion

The word compassion comes from Latin root words that mean "to bear with" or "to suffer with." Compassion often starts with empathy, but it is bigger than empathy. Compassion is an active

Make Connections

Doctors, nurses, rescue workers, social workers, and counselors need to feel empathy for the people they help. Most people in these professions pursued their lines of work because they wanted to help others. But they can also be exhausted by empathy. Not everyone they try to help will have a happy ending. Some people will continue to hurt; some people will even die. People in helping professions who get overwhelmed with their empathy may experience what's known as "burnout." If they're going to be able to do their jobs, they have to step back a little from their own emotions. They need less emotional empathy and more compassionate empathy.

concern for another person's pain; it's not just a feeling, but it's also a willingness to do whatever it takes to help the other person, to put yourself next to them and do whatever you can to lift them out of their situation. Mother Teresa, the woman who worked so hard in the slums of Calcutta, called this "love in action." It means being willing to set aside your own selfish needs and give yourself for another's good.

So in the situation with your friend, compassion is what you're feeling when you stay with her, listening to her talk, letting her cry on your shoulder. It's what makes you try to find ways to cheer her up the next day, and it's what makes you do all you can to help her get over her boyfriend.

After you see on the TV the children who are suffering in Africa, compassion is what makes you go to the Internet and find charities that are working to help those children. Compassion is what makes you decide to give part of your allowance every month to that charity.

And compassion is what makes you be nice to the kid on the bus, not just that day, but always. Whenever you pass him in the hall, you smile and say hi. You ask him to sit down with you and your friends in the cafeteria. You make sure people include him. You refuse to be one of the people who treat him as though he's weird.

Compassion changes the world. And it changes us.

CONFLICTING EMOTIONS

But empathy and compassion aren't always easy things to feel. And sometimes other feelings get in their way. Maybe you feel embarrassed to be seen with the kid on the bus. Or you feel impatient with your friend because a month later she's still feeling sad about her boyfriend, and you want her to just get over it. Or your older sister has a new smartphone, and you feel so envious that you want to use your allowance to buy one for yourself, instead of sending your money to help people in Africa.

All human beings feel things that contradict each other. It just

Make Connections

All the major religions stress that compassion is an important part of serving God. Hindus speak of ahimsa, the "God quality" within a person that creates active responses of respect, service, and care for those in need. Compassion is also a central teaching of Buddhism. Buddhist compassion—karuna—is based on the understanding that all beings are connected; my well-being depends on yours—and on the entire planet's. In the Judeo-Christian tradition, compassion is the way God interacts with creation, and it is the way people should interact with one another. Islam considers compassion to be part of Allah's very nature, one that humans are called to imitate. In each of these religious traditions, compassion is considered a religious obligation. It's the "Golden Rule" taught by each of the religions: "Love others the same way you love yourself."

comes with the package of being human! Even in a single day, you may go from loving your mom to hating her. You may wake up sad and go to bed happy. It's hard to make sense of it all. What's real? What's good and what's bad?

Emotions are just feelings. They come and go, the same way our physical feelings—like headaches and hunger pangs and sleepiness—come and go. It's a good idea to pay attention to our feelings and be aware of them, but we should also try to keep them in *perspective*. If you're furious with your sister, it doesn't mean you're a bad person. Emotions aren't bad or good; they're just feelings, the same way headaches and hunger and sleepiness are feelings.

But like headaches and hunger and sleepiness, your feelings, both positive and negative, tell you to pay attention to what's going on. They tell you that you need to do something. Maybe you

EMPATHY AND COMPASSION

Research Project

The author says that all the major religions include compassion as a major element in their teachings. Using the Internet, find reliable sites for each of the following religions: Islam, Christianity, Buddhism, Hinduism, and Judaism. Discover what the major teachings are of each religion, as well as the name of their holy writings. Summarize the teachings of each in a short paragraph, relating these teachings to the definitions of compassion given in this chapter. Next, find each of the religions' holy scriptures either online or in the library. From each religion's scripture, find a verse or short passage that relates to compassion, and include it in the paragraph that relates to that particular religion. You might search for that religion's version of the "Golden Rule." Last, write a final paragraph that compares and contrasts each religion with the others. How are they different from each other? What do they have in common?

need to try to relax or eat a sandwich or go to bed—or maybe you need to take some other action. It's what you *do* that is more important than what you *feel*. If you get so angry at your sister that you say or do hurtful things, there will be consequences to your actions. If you choose to talk about your anger, though, and try to compromise and find a solution, there will be different consequences.

When it comes to your feelings of impatience or embarrassment or envy in the situations we described earlier, you might want to think about why you're feeling those things. Once you have, you might choose to focus on your feelings of empathy and compassion instead. You can choose to act on those feelings rather than your negative emotions.

Scientists think that human beings developed the **capacity** to feel empathy and compassion because those feelings work to

Text-Dependent Questions

1. What three examples does the author give at the beginning of this chapter to introduce her topic?
2. What two sentences in the sidebar on p. 11 explain what emotions are from a scientific viewpoint?
3. Explain the Greek and Latin root words for "empathy" and "compassion."
4. List the three kinds of empathy and explain the differences between them.
5. Give two ways that compassion differs from empathy.

build society. Men and women with empathy and compassion make better fathers and mothers. People with strong empathy and compassion are able to work together better and get things accomplished. They're better friends to each other. They're more willing to help each other. They rescue each other from trouble. Sometimes they literally save each other's lives.

You can choose to focus on anger and hatred—and that's going to negatively change the way you live our life. Or you can focus on love and empathy and compassion—and that will change your life positively.

The more you learn about how your brain works when it comes to empathy and compassion, the more you'll be able to understand what's going on when you feel these emotions, and the more you'll be able to give them space in your mind. When that happens, you'll be one of the people who help make our world better for us all.

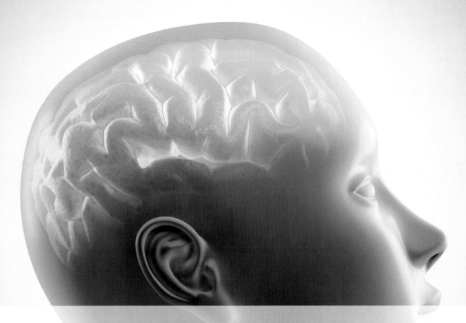

Words to Understand

neurologists: Doctors or scientists who study or treat the brain and neurons.

neuroscientist: Scientists who study the brain and nerves.

abnormalities: Strange or unexpected structures or things that could indicate a problem.

transform: Change into something else.

negative: Focusing on or having to do with the bad side of things.

positive: Focusing on or having to do with the good side of things.

activates: Switches on or causes a reaction.

nurturing: Caring for something or someone and encouraging growth and development.

meditating: Thinking deeply or focusing your mind.

participants: People who take part in something.

TWO

What Happens Inside Your Brain?

Have you ever heard someone say, "I feel your pain"? When *neurologists* do brain scans of people who are experiencing empathy and compare them to the brain scans of people who are actually suffering, they see that similar areas of the brain are activated in both. So when we feel empathy, we are actually, at some level, experiencing another's pain. We feel their pain.

We experience something a little different when we feel compassion. When you think about someone compassionate, someone like Mother Teresa or anyone who commits his life to helping others, you probably think of this person as being unusually good. Compassionate people are often deeply religious. You may think of them as having good "souls"—but you probably don't think about what's going on in their brain cells. In fact, something

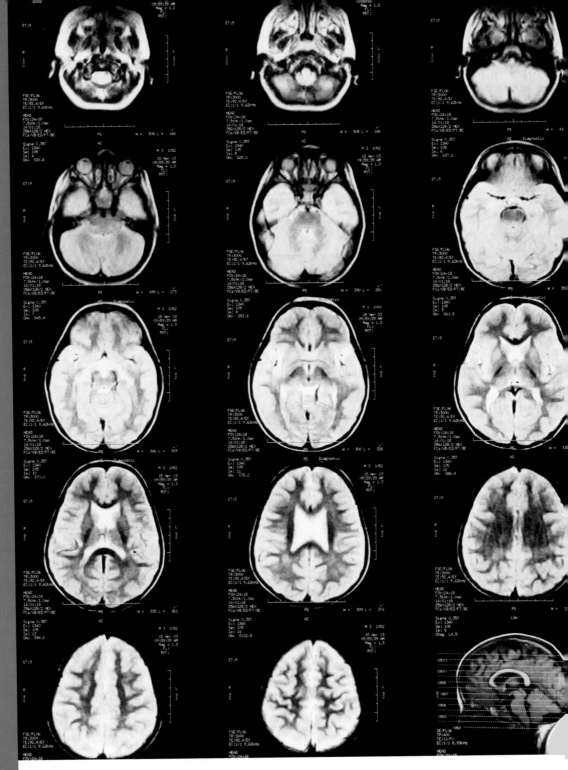

These MRI images give doctors and scientists a look inside the person's head. By doing so, they can actually see emotions taking place.

Make Connections: What Is an MRI?

 Magnetic resonance imaging (MRI) is a test that uses a magnetic field and pulses of radio wave energy to make pictures of organs and structures inside the body. For an MRI test, the area of the body being studied is placed inside a special machine that contains a strong magnet. Pictures from an MRI scan are digital images that can be saved and stored on a computer for more study.

special is going on in the brains of people who are unusually compassionate.

WHERE DO EMOTIONS TAKE PLACE?

Researchers have discovered that all our emotions—including empathy and compassion—are produced in our brains. Scientists have begun to map the human brain, identifying which parts of our brains do what. In doing so, researchers have found that human emotion is a pleasant or unpleasant mental state that's created in the limbic system of our brain.

These feelings at their most basic level have no words; they're simply sensations. However, we've learned to give them labels (such as amusement, anger, disgust, dislike, embarrassment, fear, guilt, happiness, hate, love, sadness, shame, surprise, and many others). As we experience these feelings, chemicals inside our brains are making our brain cells behave in specific ways. When scientists look at an MRI of a person's brain when she's feeling emotions, they can actually see the different parts of her brain lighting up as they become more active.

EMPATHY AND COMPASSION

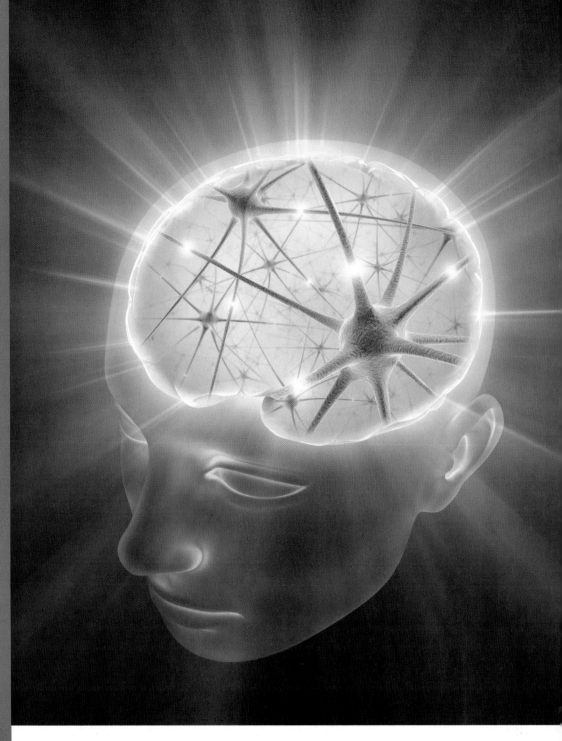

Inside your brain are millions of neurons. These cells have amazing abilities that allow you to respond to the world around you.

Make Connections: What Is the Limbic System?

The limbic system is a set of brain structures located on top of the brainstem and buried under the brain's gray matter. Limbic system structures are involved in many of our emotions, including fear, anger, and pleasure. Other structures within the limbic system are involved with memory and our sense of smell.

EMPATHY

Empathy is something that happens deep inside our brains. It's caused by a set of complicated reactions between our brain cells. Human beings aren't the only ones who experience it. Researchers have observed other primates (apes and monkeys), dogs, and even rats demonstrating empathy.

Scientists think that this emotion is caused by what they call "mirror" neurons, cells in the brain that fire when we see someone else doing something. The messages these cells send are much the same as the messages we would receive from our brains if we were in the same situation in ourselves. Our brains are acting like a mirror to another's pain or suffering.

In 2004, Dr. Tania Singer, a psychologist and *neuroscientist*, discovered that pain-sensitive parts of the brain are activated when we empathize with others who are in pain. Dr. Singer and her team of researchers used MRIs to look inside people's brains. She was able to measure the neural responses of people both when they themselves experienced pain and when a loved one, who was with them in the same room, experienced pain. In both situations, the people felt an emotional response. The people who watched while a loved one was in pain didn't actually feel pain in their bodies, but they did have the same response in their brains.

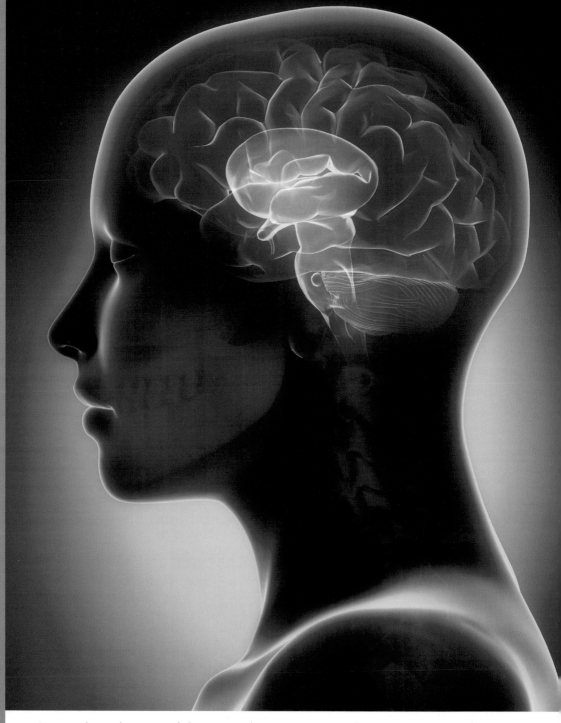

Researchers discovered that empathy is experienced in certain parts of our brains.

Research Project

This chapter refers to several research studies. Use the Internet or library to investigate how research studies are conducted. What are the elements of a good research study? Now, think of a simple study that you might do to investigate empathy and compassion in your friends and family. Obviously, you won't be able to use an MRI to look into their brains, but you can ask questions about their feelings. Be sure to include all the basic elements of a good research study. Report your findings.

Dr. Singer's research was important. It proved that human beings are connected to each other in ways we may not have suspected. We are not only controlled by self-interest. Instead, we also naturally respond to others' feelings.

Dr. Singer's research got other scientists interested. They wanted to find out more. In 2012, a team of researchers at Mount Sinai School of Medicine in New York found that one area of the brain, called the anterior insular cortex, is the activity center of human empathy, whereas other areas of the brain are not. Here's how they made this discovery.

A group of patients were shown photographs of people in pain. Some of the patients had had parts of their anterior insular cortex removed because of tumors there; another group of patients had had other parts of their brain removed; and the third group had normal brains. The first group, the group that had damaged anterior insular cortexes, were unable to look at the expressions of the people in the photographs and pick out which ones were in pain. The other two groups could.

The scientists were excited by their discovery. It proved that people with *abnormalities* in their anterior insular cortexes—whether from disease, injury, or some difference in development—have

Looking inside the brains of Buddhist monks has helped scientists better understand compassion.

less empathy than other people. This meant that people with difficulty understanding others' emotions might have parts of their brains not working normally. It also meant that the condition could possibly be treated. Maybe one day there will even be medicine that makes people feel more empathy!

But right now it's not that simple. Other researchers have found that there are ten or more parts of the brain involved in the experience of empathy. It's a complicated process. Understanding how they all interact with each other is difficult.

No one likes to feel pain. So some people may teach themselves to feel less empathy. They choose to focus on other feelings, instead of thinking about others' pain, and they numb their empathy. Another solution, however, is to **transform** empathy into compassion.

Text-Dependent Questions

1. This chapter discusses specific structures within the brain. List the names of two brain parts discussed in this chapter and explain how each is connected to empathy or compassion.
2. What evidence did Dr. Tania Singer find that human beings are naturally inclined to be compassionate?
3. This chapter explains ways that compassion differs from empathy. Summarize these differences in a sentence.
4. Referring to the sidebar on page 23, explain what an MRI does.
5. What is the evidence provided in this chapter that compassion can be taught?

COMPASSION

In an interview with the Cognitive Neuroscience Society, Dr. Singer said, "When I empathize with the suffering of others, I feel the pain of others; I am suffering myself. This can become so intense that it produces empathic distress in me and in the long run could lead to burnout and withdrawal. In contrast, if we feel compassion for someone else's suffering, we do not necessarily feel with their pain but we feel concern—a feeling of love and warmth. . . ." Dr. Singer went on to explain that the neural networks underlying empathy and compassion are very different. Whereas empathy increases *negative* emotions, compassion produces *positive* feelings of warmth. It *activates* brain networks connected with relationships and emotional reward.

To find out more about how compassion looks inside the human brain, Dr. Singer studied a group of Buddhist monks who were well known for demonstrating compassion. She took MRIs of the monks' brains while they watched videos of people suffering. The brain scans showed that the monks had activity in areas of the

Practicing certain meditation techniques could change your brain's activity, making you more compassionate.

brain that neuroscientists have proven are connected to caring for others, *nurturing* young, and forming relationships within a group. When the same videos were shown to another group of people, however, the parts of the brain that lit up were ones connected to unpleasant feelings like sadness and pain. These people were experiencing empathy but not compassion.

What made the difference? Dr. Singer discovered that the monks regularly practiced *meditating* on others' pain. One of the monks said that his meditation produced "the warm, loving caring feeling which a mother would activate towards a crying child." This made Dr. Singer wonder if people could be taught to become more like the monks. Could people train their brains to shift empathy into compassion?

Dr. Singer has found out that in fact people *can* be trained to be more compassionate. Using meditation techniques similar to the Buddhist monks', Singer and her team have managed to shift people's brain activity from areas that are more likely to cause negative feelings like sadness and pain to other areas, which are connected to relationships and nurturing behaviors. Instead of making people sad, these areas make people feel good.

In 2012, researchers at Emory School of Medicine in 2012 showed that Dr. Singer's research could be right. The Emory study taught *participants* to meditate on compassion-focused thoughts for eight weeks. At the end of that period, the participants were better able to identify others' emotions when they looked at black-and-white photographs that showed just people's eyes.

So what does that mean? How might your life be different if you could be more compassionate? How might the world be different?

Words to Understand

segregated: Seperated or divided based on membership in a group or an external characteristic, such as skin color.

role models: People on whom others base their behavior.

prejudice: Judging someone ahead of time without knowing them, often based on membership in a group or physical appearence.

discrimination: The unfair treatment of certain groups or races.

dehumanized: Treated or thought of as less than human.

ethnic group: A group determined by nationality or race, or by an external physical characteristic thought to display race (such as skin color).

genocide: The killing of an entire group or race of people.

evolved: Developed over a long time.

THREE

HOW DO EMPATHY & COMPASSION CHANGE YOUR LIFE?

You might think that your emotions are just something that come and go. They're important to you, but you don't feel like they matter much to the world outside your own head. You certainly don't feel as though they matter much to the rest of the world.

But here's the thing: your emotions are triggered by events in the world around you—but then they can make you react in ways that change your life, either positively or negatively. And emotions like empathy and compassion can change not only your own life. They can change the entire world.

MARTIN LUTHER KING, JR.

Martin Luther King, Jr., grew up in Georgia in the 1940s, during the days when prejudice kept blacks and whites separated,

EMPATHY AND COMPASSION

Martin Luther King Jr.'s compassion changed our world.

Make Connections: Who Was Gandhi?

 Mohandas Gandhi spent the first part of his life in South Africa working to fight discrimination there. When he moved back to India, his homeland, he fought for the poor people of India. He created the concept of *Satyagraha*, a nonviolent way of protesting against injustices. Gandhi said, "You must be the change you wish to see in the world."

Martin Luther King Jr., as well as many other civil rights leaders, learned from Gandhi's concept of nonviolent protest. Gandhi's compassion from others changed not only his own country, but it also continues to influence people around the world. "The best way to find yourself," he wrote, "is to lose yourself in the service of others."

especially in the South. He saw what life was like for black people in the South during that time. Black children weren't allowed to go to the same schools as white children (and most black schools lacked books, supplies, and other resources). Drinking fountains, lunch counters, and laundromats were all *segregated*. Employers could legally refuse to hire blacks for jobs. Landlords could refuse to rent houses to black people. Blacks and whites lived in separate neighborhoods, and black neighborhoods were often poor and unsafe. Often, blacks were kept from registering to vote. They didn't have many educational opportunities.

Martin's parents were educated, and his family had enough money, but he grew up feeling sorry for the people around him. But his feelings didn't stop there. His father and grandfather were active in the fight for equal rights for blacks, so Martin grew up with *role models* who taught him what compassion looks like.

During college, Martin decided to become a minister, like his father. He described his decision as an "inner urge to serve humanity." He became a pastor, and soon he became the head of the civil rights movement. His Christianity motivated him to take

Martin Luther King Jr. was inspired by Gandhi, another human being with immense compassion.

action, but so did his reading of Mohandas Gandhi, who had used nonviolent means to change India.

Martin's influence in the American civil rights movement spread to other countries. Despite having his house bombed and his life threatened, Martin never gave up. In 1963, he said, "I say to you today, my friends, so even though we face the difficulties of today and tomorrow, I still have a dream . . . that one day this nation will rise up and live out the true meaning of its creed: 'we hold these truths to be self-evident, that all men are created equal.'"

Martin ran into failures and challenges, but his compassion for others kept pushing him forward. He wrote, "I have decided to stick to love. . . . Hate is too great a burden to bear." He set aside his own needs and his own safety. "Never, never be afraid to do what's right," he wrote, "especially if the well-being of a person or animal is at stake. Society's punishments are small compared to the wounds we inflict on our soul when we look the other way."

In a speech he gave in 1968, he said, "It really doesn't matter with me now, because I've been to the mountaintop, I've seen the Promised Land." He continued, "I may not get there with you. But I want you to know tonight, that we, as a people, will get to the Promised Land." Martin lost his life for what he believed, but his words came true. Because of his compassion, laws were changed. Black Americans gained rights they had never had before. Whites learned to think about race differently. *Prejudice* and *discrimination* were pushed back. And these changes spread around the world, touching countries in Africa and Asia as well.

All because of one man's compassion.

AN ORDINARY WOMAN

Almost everyone in the world has heard of Martin Luther King Jr. In the United States, a national holiday makes sure no one forgets him. But most people have never heard of Ann Murphy. Like Martin Luther King Jr., though, Ann has taken compassionate action, and she's changing the world around her.

Ann started out by convincing the owner of a Church's Chicken

EMPATHY AND COMPASSION

When you see a homeless person in the street, do you feel sorry and look away—or do you try to think of some action you could take to help? One feeling is empathy, but the other is compassion.

Empathy is a feeling inside you, but compassion has hands.

restaurant to donate his leftover chicken for her to hand out to people who have no homes. Ann doesn't like to call them "homeless people." She told a reporter from Greensboro, North Carolina's *News & Record* that she considers these people her friends. "They're not homeless. I don't call them that because that is not who they are. I tell people, 'Two steps sideways and that could be any one of us.' That's all it takes."

Ann was in her fifties when compassion took over her life. Like Martin's compassion, Ann's is connected to her religious beliefs. She told the reporter that she said to God, "Why don't you take my life and show me what you want me to do, and I'll do that." A few weeks later, she says, she saw a front-page article with the headline "Homeless Prepare for the Bitter Cold."

Ann felt empathy, but it didn't stop there. She thought about what she could do to help cold people. Her empathy turned into compassion. She decided to talk to restaurants around Greensboro

The excitement of giving a gift can trigger even more pleasure inside a person's brain than receiving the gift would have.

and find out if their owners would be willing to donate food to help people who were cold and hungry. She started small, and went on from there to raise thousands of dollars for the people she calls her friends, people who are homeless.

Ann started out Baptist (a form of Christianity), and then she stopped believing in God at all. Today she says her religious beliefs are deep but simple. "I believe that A, God is love; B, I don't know and I don't think it matters; and C, my religion is compassion and kindness."

When you start practicing compassion—taking it from an inside feeling to an outside action—it changes the world. And it also changes you.

COMPASSION AND YOU

When you reach out to others, you make the world a better place—but you also increase your own well-being. Researchers have found that connecting with others in a meaningful way will help you have better mental and physical health. It speeds up the healing process, so you recover from injuries and illnesses faster. Compassion may even make you live longer! It turns out that the old saying "It's better to give than receive" has some truth to it. That's what researchers are discovering.

When certain parts of our brains are activated, we feel pleasure. Many things can trigger pleasure. It could be a slice of chocolate cake, a hundred-dollar bill, a kiss from a girlfriend, or your team winning the Super Bowl. And, as it turns out, compassion makes the same part of our brains go into action as pleasure does. In a brain imaging study done by neuroscientists at the National Institutes of Health, they found that when people saw others give gifts to someone, the "pleasure centers" of their brains lit up just as much as when they received the gift themselves.

The momentary pleasure isn't the end of the story. Giving to others increases our overall well-being. Elizabeth Dunn, a professor of psychology at the University of British Columbia, found that giving away money makes people happier than spending it.

Even children can learn that giving something away actually feels better than having it all to yourself.

The participants in her study (published in *Science* magazine in 2008) received a sum of money; half of them were told to spend the money on themselves, while the other half were instructed to spend the money on others. At the end of the study, the people who had spent money on others were much happier than the people who had spent money on themselves.

Apparently, even toddlers can benefit from compassion's positive effects. Another study, this one done by Lara Aknin at the University of British Columbia, showed that two-year-olds were happier when they gave away treats than they were when they kept the treats for themselves.

So if compassion feels so good, why don't we all practice it more often?

WHEN EMPATHY & COMPASSION BREAK DOWN

Sometimes we don't feel much empathy for others—and if can't feel empathy, we probably won't feel compassion either.

Say you're on the school bus and everyone is being mean to the poor kid no one likes. This time, instead of feeling empathy for him, you think to yourself, "He deserves to be picked on. If he acted like a normal person, they wouldn't be so mean to him. Look at the way he dresses! And he smells funny. No wonder no one wants to sit with him!"

These kinds of thoughts turn the boy on the bus into someone very different from you. Sociologists call this kind of thinking "in-group/out-group dynamics." You think of the people who are in you in-group as being like you, while those who are in an out-group seem very different from you—and because they're not like you, they don't seem worthy of empathy. This is the kind of thinking that might keep you from feeling compassion and empathy for the boy on the bus. It might also keep you from feeling anything for the African children you see on TV. (After all, they live on the other side of the world from you!)

During war, we'd like to believe that the "enemy" is as evil and unhuman as a science fiction alien—and that way we can feel good about killing him. In real life, though, the enemy is really another human being like you.

Text-Dependent Questions

1. This chapter provides two examples of individuals who demonstrated compassion in their lives. List what these two individuals have in common.
2. In the section headed "Compassion and You," the author provides three ways that compassion improves well-being. List them.
3. Explain how feelings of pleasure are connected to the brain.
4. Summarize in a sentence the findings of one of the studies described in this chapter.
5. Explain how the author implies that genocide is connected to in-groups and out-groups.

A sociologist would say that you've *dehumanized* the boy on the bus and the children on TV. They don't seem as human to you as members of your in-group. In your mind, they're not as important, not as valuable, not even quite as real.

This is why people who are very compassionate in one setting can be cold or even cruel in another. It's why the same person who goes out of his way to be kind to his friends can be mean to someone from another *ethnic group*. This perspective puts people into two categories: "us" and "them." It's the kind of thinking that goes on a lot in middle schools and high schools, where tight groups often form. It's also the kind of thinking that can lead to *genocide*.

Thinking in terms of in-groups and out-groups is a human tendency. Just like empathy and compassion, it's something that originally *evolved* to help human beings survive.

Imagine that you're one of the earliest human beings who lived thousands of years ago. You belong to a clan that works together to find food. The clan makes you feel stronger and safer; without the others, you know you probably wouldn't survive. When you

EMPATHY AND COMPASSION

In-group and out-group thinking shatters human compassion. This is all that's left of the more than 2 million people who died in Cambodia when the Khmer Rouge killed their "enemies."

Research Project

From your knowledge of history, pick one war or conflict (such as World War II, the civil war in the Sudan, or the ongoing tension in the Middle East). Use the Internet and the library to investigate this war or conflict further. Describe how in-group/out-group dynamics apply to this conflict. Explain how people's ideas about in-groups and out-groups contributed to the fighting. How did it lead to the breakdown of compassion?

run into other groups, you see them as a threat to you. They may fight you for food. They might hurt you. So you work together with your clan to fight off the invaders. The strangers are the out-group, and your clan is the in-group.

What started out as a way for humans to survive, though, is no longer so helpful today. We're not cave people anymore.

So what can we do?

Words to Understand

reconcile: Cause to coexist in harmony.

atrocities: Horrible or evil acts.

inhibiting: Slowing down or preventing.

belligerent: Warlike or eager to fight.

charter: A written document outlining an organization's beliefs or goals.

inviolable: Never to be broken or taken away.

sanctity: State of being extremely important and valuable.

equity: Fairness or equality of treatment.

chauvinism: Aggressive patriotism or belief that one group of people is better than another.

impoverish: Cause someone to not have enough money to survive or live safely and healthily.

exploit: Use a person in an unfair and selfish way.

denigrating: Criticizing unfairly.

illegitimate: Not allowed by the law or not approved by a country or organization.

diversity: The state of having a wide range of differences.

luminous: Shining with light.

dynamic: Energetic and positive with attitude.

transcend: Rise above.

dogmatic: Sticking to a certain set of beliefs or principles, often to the degree that you refuse to accept anything else as true.

ideological: Having to do with your beliefs, ideas, and ethics.

interdependence: A state of countries, people, or organizations relying on each other.

enlightenment: A state of having a modern, well-informed point of view, or having knowledge and wisdom.

FOUR

LEARNING FROM YOUR EMOTIONS

It's not always easy to feel empathy and compassion. Some people just don't seem very likeable. Some people have been mean to us. Sometimes the problem just seems too big that we don't want to care about it; after all, what can we do to change it?

Human beings naturally work together and are kind—and human beings also fight each other and are aggressive. How can we *reconcile* these two natural human traits? How can *you* reconcile them in your own life?

EMPATHY VS. VIOLENCE

In 2010, researchers from the University of Valencia investigated the brain structures involved with both empathy and violence. They discovered that they're the same. The parts of the brain that are activated by empathy are the same parts that violence activates.

EMPATHY AND COMPASSION

The more you take time to listen and feel empathy, the less room there will be in your brain for violent emotions.

The study's lead author, Moya Albiol, stated, "Just as our species could be considered the most violent, since we are capable of serial killings, genocide and other *atrocities*, we are also the most empathetic species, which would seem to be the other side of the coin." He added, "We all know that encouraging empathy has an *inhibiting* effect on violence, but this may not only be a social question but also a biological one—stimulation of these neuronal circuits in one direction reduces their activity in the other."

In other words, the more empathy you feel, the less likely you are to be violent. Empathy takes up the space in your brain where violence would live. It pushes the violence out. "Educating people to be empathetic could be an education for peace, bringing about a reduction in conflict and *belligerent* acts," the researcher concluded.

CHARTER FOR COMPASSION

Karen Armstrong is someone who is fighting hard to teach people to choose compassion and empathy over violence. She's an author who has written about the role compassion plays in spirituality and in the major religions. In 2008, she won a TED Prize for $100,000. She used the money to create a *charter* for compassion—and then spread it around the world. The charter has been signed by celebrities, by the Dalai Lama, and by the entire city of Seattle. By October 2013, more than 99,000 people had signed it.

Here's what the charter says:

> The principle of compassion lies at the heart of all religious, ethical and spiritual traditions, calling us always to treat all others as we wish to be treated ourselves. Compassion impels us to work tirelessly to alleviate the suffering of our fellow creatures, to dethrone ourselves from the centre of our world and put another there, and to honour the *inviolable sanctity* of every single human

The world's great religions have triggered wars and conflict—but they have also inspired people to great acts of compassion.

Make Connections:
Wise Words from Compassionate Men

A love that is based on the goodness of those whom you love is a mercenary affair.
—Gandhi

Every word and deed must contribute to an understanding with the enemy and release those vast reservoirs of goodwill which have been blocked by the impenetrable walls of hate.
—Martin Luther King, Jr.

being, treating everybody, without exception, with absolute justice, *equity* and respect.

It is also necessary in both public and private life to refrain consistently and empathically from inflicting pain. To act or speak violently out of spite, *chauvinism*, or self-interest, to *impoverish*, *exploit* or deny basic rights to anybody, and to incite hatred by *denigrating* others—even our enemies—is a denial of our common humanity. We acknowledge that we have failed to live compassionately and that some have even increased the sum of human misery in the name of religion.

We therefore call upon all men and women to restore compassion to the centre of morality and religion—to return to the ancient principle that any interpretation of scripture that breeds violence, hatred or disdain is *illegitimate*—to ensure that youth are given accurate and respectful information about other traditions, religions and cultures—to encourage a positive appreciation of cultural and religious *diversity*—to cultivate an informed empathy with the suffering of all human beings—even those regarded as enemies.

54

EMPATHY AND COMPASSION

Karen Armstrong is working hard to build a more compassionate world by telling people all around the world about the Charter for Compassion.

Research Project

To get a sense of the Charter of Compassion movement's timeline, go to the charter's website: http://charterforcompassion.org. Using information provided on the site, explain the steps that led to the charter's creation. Next, update your information by going to the Facebook page for the Charter of Compassion: https://www.facebook.com/CharterforCompassion. Summarize the information you find there in three paragraphs that answer the questions for what is happening right now: Who? What? Where? (Who is doing what where?)

We urgently need to make compassion a clear, **_luminous_** and **_dynamic_** force in our polarized world. Rooted in a principled determination to **_transcend_** selfishness, compassion can break down political, **_dogmatic_**, **_ideological_** and religious boundaries. Born of our deep **_interdependence_**, compassion is essential to human relationships and to a fulfilled humanity. It is the path to **_enlightenment_**, and indispensable to the creation of a just economy and a peaceful global community.

The Charter for Compassion organization lists twelve steps that lead to a more compassionate life. Karen Armstrong believes that by taking these steps, we retrain our brains. We make room in our brain circuits for empathy. We allow compassion to grow in our lives.

Try them out for yourself. See what you think.

Step 1: Learn About Compassion
Step 2: Look at Your Own World (Where do you see compassion in your family, group of friends, school, and country?

One side of compassion has to do with being with people, taking action to help them—but compassion is also built by spending time alone, thinking, praying, or meditating.

Text-Dependent Questions

1. In this chapter, what clues show you that human beings have the power to choose whether to be violent?

2. The first paragraph of the Charter of Compassion uses the word "dethrone." What metaphor does the word call on? Why do you think the authors of the charter chose this word?

3. The second paragraph of the Charter of Compassion lists at least four behaviors that deny our "common humanity." What are they?

4. List three examples from the Charter of Compassion that draw on an understanding of in-group/out-group dynamics' connection to empathy.

5. Rewrite in your own words each of the two quotes given by Gandhi and Martin Luther King, Jr., and explain how they connect to compassion.

Where do you see a lack of compassion? Are there areas where violence is winning out over empathy?)

Step 3: Have Compassion for Yourself (Karen Armstrong says that when we judge ourselves harshly, we are more likely to be on the defense against others, rather than experiencing empathy for them.)

Step 4: Practice Empathy (Make a conscious effort to tune into the feelings of others.)

Step 5: Mindfulness (Meditate.)

Reach out to others. The world needs you.

Step 6: Take Action (Each day, find opportunities to live out the Golden Rule.)

Step 7: Acknowledge How Little We Know (Let go of your certainties and be open to considering new points of view.)

Step 8: How Should We Speak to One Another? (Pay attention to the ways you talk to and about others. Notice when you start to reflect in-group/out-group thinking.)

Step 9: Concern for Everybody (Practice thinking of yourself as connected to the entire human race, not just the people you know or who are like you.)

Step 10: Knowledge (Learn about other cultures and religions, so that you can understand their perspectives better.)

Step 11: Recognition (Recognize where pain and suffering exists in the world.)

Step 12: Love Your Enemies (Think about the people in your life you see as a threat to you—and then think of ways to be kind to them. Practice thinking of them as human beings who are a lot like you.)

Find Out More

IN BOOKS

Bodhipaksa. *Mindfulness Meditations for Teens*. Newmarket, N.H.: Wildmind, 2010.

Boyle, Gregory. *Tattoos on the Heart: The Power of Boundless Compassion*. New York: Free Press, 2010.

The Dalai Lama. *An Open Heart: Practicing Compassion in Everyday Life*. New York: Back Bay Books, 2008.

ONLINE

Compassionate Kids
www.compassionatekids.com

Compassion International
www.compassion.com

Charter for Compassion
charterforcompassion.org

Series Glossary of Key Terms

adrenaline: An important body chemical that helps prepare your body for danger. Too much adrenaline can also cause stress and anxiety.

amygdala: An almond-shaped area within the brain where the flight-or-flight response takes place.

autonomic nervous system: The part of your nervous system that works without your conscious control, regulating body functions such as heartbeat, breathing, and digestion.

cognitive: Having to do with thinking and conscious mental activities.

cortex: The area of your brain where rational thinking takes place.

dopamine: A brain chemical that gives pleasure as a reward for certain activities.

endorphins: Brain chemicals that create feelings of happiness.

fight-or-flight response: Your brain's reaction to danger, which sends out messages to the rest of the body, getting it ready to either run away or fight.

hippocampus: Part of the brain's limbic system that plays an important role in memory.

hypothalamus: The brain structure that gets messages out to your body's autonomic nervous system, preparing it to face danger.

limbic system: The part of the brain where emotions are processed.

neurons: Nerve cells found in the brain, spinal cord, and throughout the body.

neurotransmitters: Chemicals that carry messages across the tiny gaps between nerve cells.

serotonin: A neurotransmitter that plays a role in happiness and depression.

stress: This feeling that life is just too much to handle can be triggered by anything that poses a threat to our well-being, including emotions, external events, and physical illnesses.

Index

About the Author & Consultant

Rosa Waters lives in New York State. She has worked as a writer for several years, producing works on health, history, and other topics.

Cindy Croft is director of the Center for Inclusive Child Care at Concordia University, St. Paul, Minnesota where she also serves as faculty in the College of Education. She is field faculty at the University of Minnesota Center for Early Education and Development program and teaches for the Minnesota on-line Eager To Learn program. She has her M.A. in education with early childhood emphasis. She has authored *The Six Keys: Strategies for Promoting Children's Mental Health in Early Childhood Programs* and co-authored *Children and Challenging Behavior: Making Inclusion Work* with Deborah Hewitt. She has worked in the early childhood field for the past twenty years.

Picture Credits

BOOK CHARGING CARD

Accession No. _____ Call No. _____

Author _____

Title _____

| Date Issued | Borrower's Name |